MEDIA LITERACY™

PRIVACY AND DIGITAL SECURITY

MEGAN FROMM, Ph.D.

rosen publishing's
rosen central®

NEW YORK

Published in 2015 by The Rosen Publishing Group, Inc.
29 East 21st Street, New York, NY 10010

First Edition

Library of Congress Cataloging-in-Publication Data

Fromm, Megan, author.
Privacy and digital security/Megan Fromm.—First edition.
    pages cm.—(Media literacy)
Includes bibliographical references and index.
ISBN 978-1-4777-8068-8 (library bound)
1. Computer security—Juvenile literature. 2. Information technology—Security measures—Juvenile literature. 3. Digital media—Security measures—Juvenile literature. 4. Data protection—Juvenile literature. I. Title.
QA76.9.A25F76 2015
005.8—dc23

2014015938

Manufactured in Malaysia

CONTENTS

Former National Security Agency contractor Edward Snowden handed over thousands of classified documents to international newspapers.

INTRODUCTION

When former Central Intelligence Agency employee and National Security Agency contractor Edward Snowden released hundreds of thousands of classified documents in 2013, concern immediately shifted to the security of America's most important intelligence documents. But Snowden's leak raised other important questions, including how a journalist—or any other person acting in the interest of public disclosure—can maintain privacy and security in the pursuit of truth.

As more journalists and citizens turn to the seemingly anonymous masses of the Internet to release information, the safety and security of both journalists and sources becomes not just a scene from some futuristic dystopian thriller, but a reality with significant consequences.

Take, for example, the case of Private First Class Bradley Manning, who was sentenced in 2013 to 35 years in prison for the largest leak of classified documents in U.S. history.[1] Manning, who networked with WikiLeaks founder Julian Assange to release the documents, was declared both a hero and an enemy of the state.

Among the information Manning released to WikiLeaks was a video showing footage of a U.S. helicopter in Baghdad opening fire on a group of people who were neither confirmed innocents nor confirmed insurgents. Iraqi children and two journalists died in the firefight.

In a statement following the sentencing, Manning explained the risk taken to release information he felt was vital for citizens to know: "I will serve my time knowing that sometimes you have to pay a heavy price to live in a free society."[2]

Both Manning and Snowden represent high-profile cases, but their stories are not unique. They represent a

U.S. Army Pfc. Bradley Manning was convicted of espionage in 2013 for giving classified documents to WikiLeaks. He was sentenced to thirty-five years in prison with eligibility for parole after seven.

shifting communication environment in which the benefits of emerging technology are also the Achilles' heel in a country that strives to strike a balance between freedom, independence, and security.

Also in 2013, Scripps Howard News Service journalists were accused of felony hacking after finding a security flaw in a major company's website that disclosed personal consumer information such as social security numbers and addresses.[3] In an article for the *Huffington Post*, reporter Isaac Wolf explained how he and fellow reporters used simple Google searches to locate telephone records and files that should have been safe behind firewalls and protected by passwords.

"Everything we saw was freely posted online, and not password protected," Wolf said. While the reporters have yet to be formally charged with a crime, the confusion over what qualifies as investigative reporting and what might be Internet hacking is worrisome for journalists everywhere.

PROTECTING INFORMATION, PROTECTING SOURCES

Today's technology and information climate is multifaceted, and protecting both the public's right to know and a journalist's right to publish is becoming infinitely more complicated. As communication becomes less linear, and the line from producer to consumer is blurred or redirected, it's more difficult to distinguish motives and to decide who is best honoring the true intentions of traditional journalism: to keep the public informed.

For example, in early 2014, federal prosecutors moved to drop data trafficking charges against a UK journalist who published a hyperlink containing hacked information in a chat room.[4] Journalist Barrett Brown was using crowdsourced information in a chat room he set up to investigate breaches in the intelligence contracting business. In doing so, he republished a hyperlink—one already published on the Internet—that prosecutors alleged constituted data trafficking because the link was related to stolen credit card information.

Geoffrey King, Internet advocacy coordinator for the Committee to Protect Journalists, described the charges against Brown as chilling for all journalists: "By seeking to put Brown in prison for linking to publicly-available, factual information, the U.S. government sends an ominous message to journalists who wish to act responsibly by substantiating their reporting."[5]

CROWDSOURCED, BUT LEGAL?

This kind of crowdsourced information is especially troublesome because courts have yet to confer on what type of crowdsourcing constitutes legally obtained information for journalists. In the past, journalists who published legally obtained classified information— that is, the journalists did not steal or otherwise illicitly obtain the information—did not face criminal prosecution. Today, cases like what Brown is facing bring such transactions under new scrutiny.

However, that has not stopped major publications from turning to crowd-sourcing. For instance, in 2010, WikiLeaks used it to help sift through tens of thousands of documents related to the war in Afghanistan leaked to the website, according to an article by Niraj Chokshi in *The Atlantic*.

Similarly, the *Guardian* in the United Kingdom solicited input from its readers regarding what leads to follow in investigating the war documents.[6] In 2011, Freedom of Information Act requests from different newspapers resulted in the release of twenty-four thousand pages of politician Sarah Palin's e-mails. The *Guardian* once again turned to crowdsourcing to ask readers for help scanning and uploading all of the e-mails to the newspaper's website. As of early 2014, more than twenty-one thousand pages of e-mails had been scanned and uploaded to the website.[7]

Publications that do choose to use crowdsourcing as a means of acquiring or sifting through information should take care to ensure that the work of the masses is downloaded legally and ethically, Jeremy Caplan at the Poynter Institute wrote. If the information was not legally obtained (as in the case of

Information wants to be free.

WikiLeaks

Founded by Julian Assange, WikiLeaks is the largest "whistleblower" website for leaked classified information. The site has posted thousands of documents related to the wars in Iraq and Afghanistan and secret intelligence operations.

some government leaks), the publications will have significant legal concerns. But even if the information came from legitimate means, such as an information request, IRS and business regulations that govern how a company can out-source what might amount to free labor still exist.[8]

For example, Caplan posed some questions that have yet to be legally or ethically answered, including this significant consideration: "How will legal authorities categorize claims against news sites from disgruntled reader-contributors dissatisfied with their authorial designation, their compensation, or the use of their intellectual property?"

UNCHARTED TERRITORY

Legal precedent has been relatively slow to adapt to changing online tech-nologies and the new role journalists have adopted, thanks to the Internet. However, initial rulings about what information revealed via the Internet—and from what sources—is subject to protection suggests that those journalists who continue to publish online in a manner reflective of traditional journalistic norms will continue to be protected.

In 2006, the California Courts of Appeal ruled that there is no difference in shield law protections between online journalistic blogging and traditional media, so online journalists are under no greater burden to reveal their

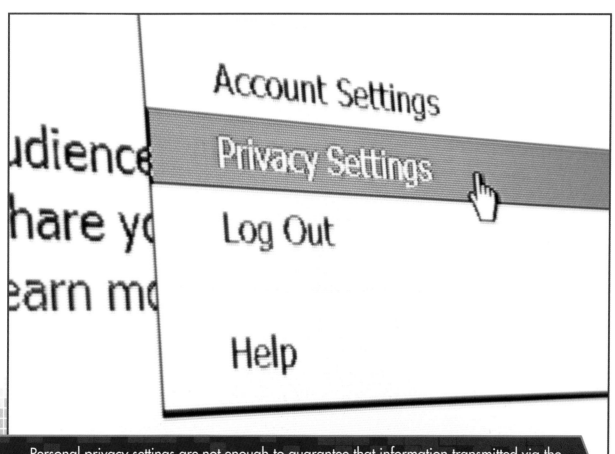

Personal privacy settings are not enough to guarantee that information transmitted via the Internet is confidential. Citizens should be sure to read privacy and disclosure statements for the websites they frequent most.

sources than print journalists.[9] Those online publishers who are perceived to operate in a manner not consistent with journalistic norms (those who fall decisively in the "blogger" category) have more to worry about, especially after an Illinois judge ruled in 2012 that a blogger for a technology website had no right to claim shield law protections.[10]

In this case, a blogger used information from an anonymous source to publish information and images related to an as-yet unreleased cell phone model. Accusing the blogger of publishing trade secrets, the cell phone's manufacturing company sought the identity of the blogger's source. Cook County Circuit Court judge Michael R. Panter ruled that the blogger could not claim journalistic protection of the source's identity because the website, TechnoBuffalo.com, did not qualify as a news medium.[11]

This and other recent legal rulings confuse an already complicated digital landscape, but they make one thing quite clear: journalists can no longer guarantee their sources are protected and anonymous when need be. To hedge their bets, some journalists are turning to encryption, anonymous web browsing, and other higher-level security measures to protect their information and sources.

CHAPTER TWO

DIGITAL SECURITY FOR JOURNALISTS

Digital security has become such an important area of expertise for journalists that professionals and institutes are scrambling to figure out how to teach the essential skills. Protecting information and sources now also means protecting oneself, so journalists can no longer be too careful about safeguarding their communications. As PBS's Susan McGregor described it:

"For American journalists, the work of Edward Snowden and Glenn Greenwald should arguably have had a two-fold impact on their digital security practice. The first stems from the awareness that many of the communication channels we use regularly when working with sources are not really protected from government surveillance, either legally or technically. The second comes from the appreciation that from here on out, understanding digital security may be a prerequisite for getting access to the really big stories," McGregor wrote for PBS's Idea Lab.[12]

McGregor argued that even while most journalists will never deal with global-conspiracy-level stories such as the Snowden leak, many journalists have sources for whom sharing information is a high-stakes game with tangible personal and professional risks.

SECURING E-MAIL AND DATA SEARCHES

Keeping e-mail secure is an essential task of journalists and data companies in the twenty-first century. Because plain-text e-mail is generally transmitted between servers over unsecured transfer points, security experts—and, more importantly, law enforcement officials—know that anything sent in such a format is subject to hacking or monitoring. While the threat of e-mail interception might sound extreme, the reality is that journalists and sources across the world have already suffered the consequences of information falling into the wrong hands.

In late 2011, British journalist and filmmaker Sean McAllister was captured in Syria after interviewing many dissidents on film. His laptop, phone, and documents seized, McAllister had no way to protect the sources he hoped to keep safe, and many of those who claim they were in touch with McAllister have fled the country for fear of retaliation.[13]

Journalists who hope to encrypt their e-mails as a means of protecting themselves and their sources can evaluate a few basic options that require only slight technical expertise, according to Jeremy Barr at the Poynter Institute. Different encryption programs and e-mail clients are available for both PC users and Mac users. PGP, which stands for Pretty Good Privacy, is a data encryption program that has been popular for more than a decade, Barr reported. Essentially, the program requires authorized users to have encryption and decryption keys that authenticate who is or is not allowed access to certain data.

"While these tools can up your privacy game, nothing is foolproof, especially when your communications are pursued by the government," Barr cautioned.[14]

British filmmaker Sean McAllister was captured in Syria after working on a documentary about dissidents. His laptop and documents were seized, and some of his sources fled the country for fear of identification and retaliation.

To keep your browser information safe, many security experts recommend using Tor, a browser program that allows for private network and browser usage. As Tor staffers explain, the program is designed to protect users against traffic analysis surveillance. According to the Tor Project homepage, "Tor helps to reduce the risks of both simple and sophisticated traffic analysis by distributing your transactions over several places on the Internet, so no single point can link you to your destination. The idea is similar to using a twisty, hard-to-follow route in order to throw off somebody who is tailing you—and then periodically erasing your footprints. Instead of taking a direct route from source to destination, data packets on the Tor network take a random pathway through several relays that cover your tracks so no observer at any single point can tell where the data came from or where it's going."[15]

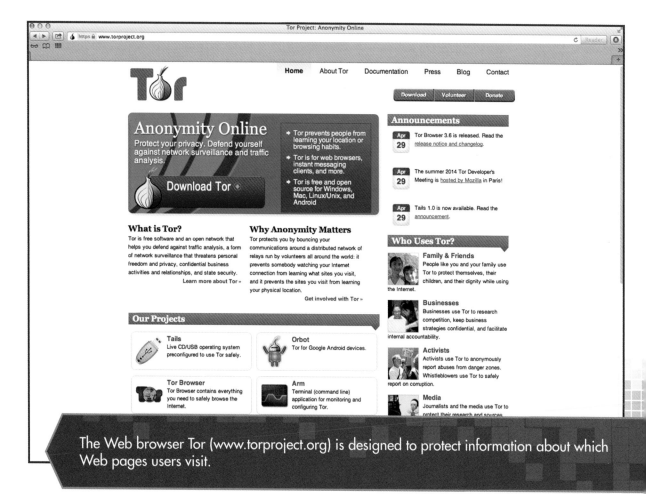

The Web browser Tor (www.torproject.org) is designed to protect information about which Web pages users visit.

The Tor Project and its services are not immune to digital vulnerabilities, however. Because it is open-source software, users of all types are constantly contributing to the code, potentially making it stronger and safer. But the same process that makes Tor so ideal is also a weakness; users could theoretically insert malicious code into the system.

In a 2013 article in the *Columbia Journalism Review,* journalist Lauren Kirchner explained how Tor has been subject to repeated attempts by the National Security Agency to crack its code, but that such attempts have been thus far unsuccessful.[16] Citing documents leaked by Edward Snowden, Kirchner and journalists from the *Washington Post* have detailed the NSA's attempts to infiltrate the Tor network:

"The NSA has mounted increasingly successful attacks to unmask the identities and locations of users of Tor. In some cases, the agency has succeeded in blocking access to the anonymous network, diverting Tor users to insecure channels. In others, it has been able to 'stain' anonymous traffic as it enters the Tor network, enabling the NSA to identify users as it exits," wrote *Washington Post* journalists Barton Gellman, Craig Timberg, and Steven Rich.[17]

Ironically, the same article describes how the State Department trains political activists around the globe on the use of Tor as a means of communicating safely and anonymously across unsecured networks.

SECURING SMARTPHONE CONNECTIONS

Like Internet browsers on a laptop or desktop computer, smartphones also use networks and servers to bounce data between points. Today, many smartphones are even linked to a user's e-mail account, meaning the browsing you do on your laptop with a browser is also logged as activity on your phone's browser. So, journalists should take care to protect mobile networks in the same way they might protect communications originating from their laptop or home computer.

Journalists and privacy-conscious citizens should safeguard information sent and received via their smartphones in the same way they protect data on a laptop or home computer.

Tor provides mobile applications that allow users privacy options across their mobile browser, a Tor-specific search engine and chat function, and via Twitter.[18] But simply using an anonymous network to browse or communicate may not stop your cell phone from recording and sending information about you to your data carrier.

To better understand how your mobile network operator tracks and receives information from your mobile phone, it's important to know a little bit about the mechanisms through which data are sent. Some key vocabulary to know include[19]:

(continued on the next page)

(continued from the previous page)

IMEI: International mobile equipment identity. This is akin to a serial number for your phone that links your phone to the network.

IMSI: International mobile subscriber identity. This is a unique number that identifies the mobile user according to country and network.

When mobile phone users send a text or make a phone call, the IMEI and IMSI data are included in each transaction, making it easy for a network operator to pinpoint the originator of a message. Why does this matter? For journalists, it represents a potential breach of security, as Lindsay Beck, a mobile security trainer and program officer on the Information and Communications Technology Team at the National Democratic Institute, explained: "When reaching out via mobile phone to a contact that is highly monitored (or if you as a journalist are under surveillance), this data can be retrieved and potentially used against you, either through legal mechanisms, intelligence or government requests for data, or extra-legal mechanisms."

One of the most common ways to increase source and user security when using mobile phones is to use what Beck called a burner phone, or a prepaid, low-tech phone that is kept separate from a journalist's main phone and is used only discreetly and in high-need situations.

THE POLITICS OF SECURITY

Digital security, surveillance, and online hacking are increasingly entrenched in current domestic and international politics. Legislation is scrambling to catch up with emerging technology, and the ever-changing ethical standards of the digital age make for an often vicious, ongoing debate about what sorts of security mechanisms infringe upon freedom of information and communication.

Headquartered at Ft. Meade in Maryland, the National Security Agency came under scrutiny after Edward Snowden's classified document leak exposed its secret phone and Internet surveillance program.

In part, changes in the global security landscape have prompted changes in technology and digital security, and threats of terrorism or breaches of national security are often cited as a reason for keeping data private or for mandating that journalists hand over sources and information.

Because there are no specific laws protecting the privacy of e-mail, some secure e-mail servers, like the defunct Lavabit, have resorted to closing up shop instead of handing over sensitive information to the FBI.[20] Unfortunately, when the government deems information sensitive or pertinent to issues of national security, there are no real mechanisms to protect a journalist from giving up that information if he or she possesses it. Likewise, government information can be withheld from journalistic inquiries simply because it falls under the national security exemption of the Freedom of Information Act.[21]

Such policies are even more complicated because they often intersect with law related to online communications and privacy. Typically, when citizens disclose information online or hand over personal data to companies, they give up certain rights to privacy because they've voluntarily placed information in the hands of a third party (this is an overly simplistic application of the third-party doctrine). In the case of electronic communications, Internet service providers and social media platforms are often perceived to be third parties. Such disclosures to third parties are not typically protected

Facebook founder Mark Zuckerberg has often told reporters that he strives to make Facebook's security settings responsive to customers' needs. But some critics say privacy and social media will always be at odds.

by court privacy rulings that tend to invoke the Fourth Amendment, which relies on a more stringent interpretation of privacy laws that references literal spaces (like a person's home).

In 2013, however, a New Jersey federal court ruled that a Facebook user's wall posts were indeed private even though they were stored via the third party of Facebook's servers. The court ruled that the posts were protected under the federal Stored Communications Act, which was created in 1986 to help protect the privacy of certain electronic communications.[22] Lawyers argue that a crucial aspect in the success of this case was that the user's profile settings had been set to the highest privacy limitations, meaning only the user's friends could see content.

Future court rulings should help to define the true nature of online privacy and what users can expect from both government and third-party data seekers.

CHAPTER THREE

WHEN IT PAYS TO BE SKEPTICAL

The high levels of paranoia regarding surveillance exhibited by whistleblowers like Edward Snowden and Bradley Manning are not entirely unfounded, some journalism experts are beginning to believe. And making journalists aware of the real threat such surveillance poses to their livelihood is a new mission for people like Steve Doig, a professor at Arizona State University's Walter Cronkite School of Journalism and Mass Communication.

Doig consistently teaches his students about security vulnerabilities for journalists through a lecture he calls Spycraft Powerpoint. The gist of the lecture? Be skeptical about exactly how confidential you think your communications really are.[23]

For example, many different investigations into Skype, a common video chat program used internationally, have raised concerns about whether the software is secure enough to prevent hacking and government monitoring. According to classified documents among those in the Snowden leak, the

With millions of users around the world, Skype is one of the most popular video chat programs on the market. However, security breaches have made journalists wonder whether it is a safe means of communicating with sources.

NSA has the ability to monitor Skype audio calls and can also collect data and information from Skype video calls and chat exchanges.[24]

Other experts estimate that a person's e-mail or online communications are never really safe from external review or malicious surveillance. When Silent Circle, a firm offering secure e-mail and communication encryption, suddenly stopped offering secure e-mail services in 2013, CEO Mike Janke said the decision was in response to insurmountable flaws inherent in e-mail communication.

"There are far too many leaks of information and metadata intrinsically in the e-mail protocols themselves," Janke said in an interview with the *Technology Review* at the Massachusetts Institute of Technology.

DATA MINING

Facebook messages and exchanges might be unsecured, but they are more likely to be used for commercial data mining than government surveillance. Data mining is a process companies use to gather massive amounts of user data, including age, race, sex, income, location, and purchasing habits. A lawsuit filed against Facebook in early 2014 in California alleges the social media company monitors users' chat messages and passes on user information to advertisers who use the information to better tailor their marketing

Facebook, like many other websites, uses algorithms and cookies to track user input, generating personalized ads that are both embedded in the content stream and placed as sidebars along the edges of the page.

approaches.[25] Facebook's terms of service disclose that the company "may enable access to public information that has been shared through our services. We may allow service providers to access information so they can help us provide services."[26]

While seemingly less alarming than unauthorized or secret surveillance, data mining is no less problematic for today's journalists and any digital consumer. Google's Street View project, in which millions of roads are mapped panoramically using a special camera and car setup, also allegedly inadvertently collected data on thousands of citizens across thirty countries by scanning Wi-Fi networks as its camera-enabled cars drove around. The data gathered during this process comprised e-mails, passwords, instant messages, and other online interactions.[27]

Data mining is also in use by government entities, as revealed in part by the Snowden leaks. In fact, the legality of the NSA's mass data collection of phone records, including numbers called, dates, and times, is currently up for debate after a U.S. district court ruled in late 2013 that the methods were unconstitutional.[28]

STUDENT DATA IS A PRIME TARGET

Students should be particularly aware that their data, including educational and demographic information, is highly valued by commercial companies. This data, commonly gathered by school districts upon enrollment, could be sold to companies or even downloaded illegally when schools contract with third-party data centers to store the information.[29]

A 2013 report by professors at Fordham Law School found that many districts do not explicitly spell out what third-party data centers can or cannot do with sensitive student data.[30] Researchers discovered that many school districts that store student data on third-party cloud servers do not use agreements that provide for data security, and some even allow vendors to retain student data. Among their main findings: "Districts frequently surrender control of student information when using cloud services: fewer than 25% of the agreements specify the purpose for disclosures of student information, fewer than 7% of the contracts restrict the sale or marketing of student information by vendors, and many agreements allow vendors to change the terms without notice."

But why is student data so lucrative? Because students—especially teenagers—are prime targets for retail marketers, and educational data present opportunities for companies to produce and sell a range of educational material targeted at specific student needs.

Website URLs that start with "https" instead of just "http" use higher levels of encryption, so the information you send and receive on these sites is more likely to be protected.

Some parents are beginning to bring legal action against school districts that use third-party data storage services perceived to be less than adequate. In New York, for example, parents filed suit in November 2013 to keep school districts from partnering with inBloom, a nonprofit student database company that is supported by millions of dollars in funds from organizations like the Carnegie Corporation of New York and the Bill & Melinda Gates Foundation.[31]

Opponents of the data organization, according to the *Washington Post* education reporter Valerie Strauss, argue that the database's seemingly monolithic nature is troublesome. The digital database would hold information about students' learning disabilities, teacher assessments, and health records, among other data.[32] Having too much information in one place sets a dangerous precedent, parents have argued, and a breach of this data could be disastrous for students' futures.

CHAPTER FOUR

TEACHING CYBER-SECURITY

Because the need for cybersecurity skills and awareness is increasing by the minute, some schools and institutions are designing cybersecurity training protocols for journalists.

Medill's National Security Zone published a "Digital Security Basics for Journalists" guide designed by security specialist Frank Smyth, executive director of consulting group Global Journalist Security. Among his basic recommendations, Smyth advocates that all journalists use licensed and updated software, invest in antivirus and antispyware software, and never let their technological devices out of their sight.[33]

The Committee to Protect Journalists uses a "Journalist Security Guide," also written by Smyth, to illustrate the many dangers of communicating online without intentional safeguards.[34] More important, CPJ advocates for a simple, personalized approach to digital security, one not so onerous that it keeps journalists from practicing basic security measures. The guide explains: "There's no point in surrounding yourself with computer security that you don't use, or that fails to address a weaker link elsewhere. Take advantage of what you know well: the people who are most likely to take offense or otherwise target your work, and what they may be seeking to obtain or disrupt. Use that knowledge to determine what you need to protect and how."

Ultimately, journalists who are aware of the threats to their person, their data, or their sources will be better equipped to protect themselves when necessary. Still, some schools and professors are reluctant to teach high levels of digital security to all journalism students as a whole, arguing that only a fraction of journalists will ever need such tools.[35] Instead, many of these professors argue that a cyber-security-oriented mind-set with just a touch of paranoia will go far in protecting the average journalist.

"It's a way of thinking: about how to evaluate the risks at hand, and how to address them in the most efficient way," journalist Lauren Kirchner wrote about the need for increased digital security awareness.

BEST PRACTICES FOR DIGITAL SECURITY

Sandra Ordonez, an outreach manager for the Open Internet Tools Project, highlights a few simple steps journalists can take to protect themselves and their sources. Those steps include:

- Encrypt your hard drive.
- Use strong passphrases.
- Enable two-step verification on phones and other apps.
- Keep social media settings as secure as possible.
- Use https whenever possible.[36]

Let's look at each of these basic steps for digital security in turn. First, encrypting your hard drive means that anyone seeking access to the information stored there would be required to present a decryption key provided

(continued on the next page)

(continued from the previous page)

to them. This is a relatively easy way to protect information on a laptop or home computer.

Ordonez emphasizes that the new term for passwords has become "passphrases," precisely to indicate how long and intricate a password should be. Short passwords are just not secure, and Ordonez claims many online users' passwords are even discernable through a bit of Facebook sleuthing.

Two-step verification is a simple method for protecting your communications. This process requires your e-mail system to send a code to your cell phone upon your initial login attempt. Without the code, an unauthorized

A Blackphone, displayed at the Mobile World Congress in Spain, automatically encrypts messages sent from the device.

user would not be able to log in to your e-mail even if he or she had obtained your password.

Maintaining high security settings on your social media accounts can be a pain because many of these policies and settings are constantly changing. But, by restricting your social media accounts to only the smallest network possible, you can strengthen your digital security.

Finally, journalists and digitally savvy citizens should stick to using websites that offer https settings. When you see this (as opposed to just http) at the beginning of a website address, you'll know the site is encrypting your communication with that page, including sensitive information such as usernames and passwords.

These are just a few of the basic best practices journalists and digital citizens can use to better protect themselves in an online world.

THE FUTURE OF SECURE TECHNOLOGY

In the aftermath of colossal information leaks across the globe, some technology companies are scrambling to offer secure, encryption-enabled devices that promise high levels of user confidence. In early 2014, a Switzerland-based company released the Blackphone, a roughly $600 smartphone that automatically encrypts communications and enables anonymous web browsing and searching.[37]

A Las Vegas company, ESD America, is now producing what it touts as a "spy-resistant phone," the CryptoPhone. For $3,500, customers whose ultimate priority is privacy can purchase the ultra-secure phone, which encrypts data, but the device is secure only when communicating with another CryptoPhone.[38]

Internet companies are also responding to increasing consumer demands for more secure data. Google has upgraded its infrastructure so users now connect only via https instead of the less-secure http connection, according to a March 2014 official Gmail blog.[39] Gmail's security engineer lead Nicolas Lidzborski wrote, "This ensures that your messages are safe not only when they move between you and Gmail's servers, but also as they move between Google's data centers—something we made a top priority after last summer's revelations."

Unfortunately, these levels of encryption apply only when communications remain inside Gmail's network, so an e-mail from a Gmail account to a Yahoo! user or Microsoft consumer might still travel on an http connection. Both Yahoo! and Microsoft have stated their intent to introduce similar security features across their e-mail platforms.[40]

CHAPTER FIVE

AN INTERVIEW WITH CYBERSECURITY EXPERT BROCK WOOD

Position/Employer: Cyberspace Operations Officer, United States Air Force
Degrees: A.S. Information Systems, B.S. Computer Information Systems
Certifications: Comptia Network+, Comptia Security+, GIAC-certified incident handler
Training: Air Force computer operations technical training, Air Force undergraduate cyber training, Air Force intermediate network warfare training
Experience: 10 years cyber operations specialist/network administrator

How are digital communications like e-mail or chats subject to surveillance by third parties or the government?

Digital communications are passed from source to destination via a complex web of private and public infrastructure to include phone lines, cable lines, and wireless transmitters. The mediums are all connected by routers that can—and often do—save logs of the source of information they receive, where that information is headed, and the actual information that was transmitted. This may sound nefarious, but whoever owns and operates each portion of this network is responsible for maintaining its functionality. Most logs are not intended as surveillance; rather they serve to troubleshoot technical problems that may (and often do) occur and, due to storage limits, the logs are typically deleted after a short period of time.

Third parties, to include governments, have the capability to either inject themselves between the source and destination to capture live transmissions or else retrieve logs from the routers that information passed through along the way. Wireless, or Wi-Fi, communications are the most susceptible as they function by broadcasting information into the open airwaves. While this information is intended for one access point, for example your home wireless router, anyone listening within miles can capture all of this digital traffic. Although hacking, or forcing yourself into an otherwise secure communication, is typically illegal without a warrant, listening in on these publicly broadcast transmissions is not.

To put it in perspective, imagine you are having a conversation with someone who is inside your house. It would be illegal for a third party to sneak in through a window so they can overhear you, but if you are shouting as loud as you can, they are within their rights to stand on the sidewalk and overhear whatever they can. Wireless communications are always shouting at anyone who will listen. It is possible, and often the practice, to encrypt wireless communications to protect them from eavesdroppers, but this is not always the case, and encryption is not always a guarantee of security.

How confident should the average e-mail user feel regarding the privacy of his or her communications? Should the average person be afraid of being hacked or having his or her e-mail read by unauthorized users? The average user should not feel very confident that they have privacy in their communications. Many service providers offer to encrypt e-mail transmissions between the user's computer and their e-mail servers, but not all give this by default. Within most businesses, and with some public e-mail providers, e-mails are transmitted in plain text, which does not contain any privacy measures. Even the computer itself cannot be fully trusted. Most people do not practice good home security by keeping their operating system patched or installing and updating antivirus software. Casual Internet browsing (or a direct hacking attack) can easily result in a spyware infection that can capture and record every keystroke on a computer.

The average user is not properly trained and equipped to know when their privacy has been compromised, but even when you have taken all precautions and security measures, you are but one small piece of a much larger puzzle that is out of your control. For every sender of e-mail, there is a receiver. How good are their security measures? Let us assume that they, too, take all precautions. As previously mentioned, every e-mail you send travels along a very complex pathway, leaving copies all along the way. Even if a system has not been hacked, it is only law, policy, and sometimes just human decency (rather than capability) that prevents a network steward from reading e-mail transmissions. No, average users should not feel any "confidence" regarding their privacy.

However, just as anyone's home could easily be broken into, statistically the chances are slim for most people. There is more information than you can fathom being transferred around the Internet at any one time, but digital storage capacities are limited, as are people who might actively monitor or review logs. There are only so many warrants, network technicians, and hackers. Although anyone's privacy can be compromised almost at a whim, the chances of the average user being targeted is slim because there is just too little to be gained. If you do have a legitimate reason to be targeted, the more security the better.

How does basic encryption work, and when is it useful?

In very general terms, encryption is like placing your message in a locked box. This does not prevent your box from being intercepted; just like all other digital communications, this locked box is still stored in countless locations and can be monitored. However, only someone with the matching key can open that box and read what is inside. In more technical terms, all information sent digitally is converted to 0s and 1s in a fashion that is easy to decipher. Encryption scrambles those 0s and 1s until they are gibberish, but it does so using a mathematical formula that can be very simply reversed only if you have the "key." There are many forms of encryption, and some are easier to break than others, but all can be broken, given enough time and resources. The best forms of encryption would take a lifetime to decode, rendering the information pointless by the time it's legible.

Encryption is not only applied to information that is moving across the Internet. It is also good practice to encrypt data at rest on a hard drive. If a hard drive were lost or stolen, that data being encrypted should make the information on the drive useless. This technique is not applied as often as it should be, and it's important to note that while a lot of Internet traffic, like e-mails, is encrypted when being sent, it is not necessarily encrypted when it arrives and is stored on the e-mail server.

How does anonymous web browsing work, and when is it useful?

While web browsing, your identity is tracked using your Internet protocol (IP) address. Every electronic device that connects to a network is assigned one of these addresses, and that address is attached to everything you do on the Internet. Not just e-mails and similar messaging; I mean literally everything. When you visit a website, your IP address is sent to that website. That is how the website knows where to send information so you can view it.

Anonymous web browsing is when a third party's IP address is given instead of your own. You tell the third party that you want to visit a website or perform an action on the Internet. The third party visits the website for you, collects the information, then sends it to your computer. Your IP address never touches the website, essentially giving you anonymity. I say essentially because everything has loopholes. Most anonymous web browsing services keep "service logs," which maintain a record of what IP address of theirs was used in place of yours, so putting those pieces together can remove anonymity.

Private browsing is very commonly used by criminals to obscure their identities for countless purposes, to include collaborating on future crimes, hacking, trading child pornography, and very commonly for downloading (or "pirating") movies, music, and software. Certainly not all use of private browsing is criminal. I personally use an anonymous web service as another layer of home network security. If my home browsing is captured by a would-be hacker or identity thief, it is not my home IP address that they are now targeting.

Journalists sometimes face situations in which the government believes their information or sources are pertinent to national security needs. How might a journalist navigate the line between freedom of information and national concerns?

Our laws and regulations are constantly evolving as we attempt to understand the complex relationship between the need to share and access information and our need to protect it. My best suggestion would be to keep up-to-date on laws as they develop, and to actually read and understand terms of service and how those services are provided, knowing what can be legally collected and how it is transmitted and stored. If you take only risks you are willing to accept, you are less likely to have undesired consequences.

GLOSSARY

BROWSER A program used to navigate the Internet and display web content.

CRYPTOGRAPHY The art and science of writing or solving codes.

ENCRYPTION Converting information into a code, often numerical, alpha-betical, or both.

FREEDOM OF INFORMATION ACT Federal legislation allowing citizens, including journalists, to request access to government records.

HACKER A person who gains unauthorized access to computer systems and databases.

HTTP Hypertext transfer protocol provides baseline standards, or protocols, that define how messages are formatted and transmitted across the Internet.

HTTPS Hypertext transfer protocol secure is an encrypted version of tradi-tional http.

IMEI International Mobile Equipment Identity is akin to a serial number for your phone that links your phone to the network.

IMSI International mobile subscriber identity is a unique number that identifies a mobile user according to country and network.

ISP Internet service provider, or a company that provides Internet access services.

PGP Pretty Good Privacy, an encryption and decryption program that secures information before, during, and after transit.

PLAIN TEXT Text that is not written in code.

ROUTER A device that joins multiple networks together.

TOR PROJECT Free software that enables anonymous web browsing by using layers of encryption and random network relay points.

WIKILEAKS An online website that publishes leaks, classified documents, and other data received from anonymous sources.

Electronic Frontier Foundation (EFF)
815 Eddy Street
San Francisco, CA 94109
(415) 436-9333
Website: http://www.eff.org
EFF describes itself as the leading nonprofit organization defending civil
    liberties around the world, especially those related to technology devel-
    opment and free expression.

SANS Institute
8120 Woodmont Avenue, Suite 205
Bethesda, MD 20814
(301) 654-7267
Website: http://www.sans.org
The SANS Institute is a premier information security training corporation with
    a larger repository of research related to digital security.

Tor Project
7 Temple Street, Suite A
Cambridge, MA 02139-2403
(781) 948-1982
Website: http://www.torproject.org
Tor Project is a nonprofit organization that builds and maintains a network of
    anonymous servers to allow for secure web browsing.

WEBSITES

Because of the changing nature of Internet links, Rosen Publishing has devel-
oped an online list of websites related to the subject of this book. This site is
updated regularly. Please use this link to access the list:

http://www.rosenlinks.com/MEDL/Priv

FOR FURTHER READING

Ahearn, Frank M., and Eileen C. Horan. *How to Disappear: Erasing Your Digital Footprint*. Guilford, CT: Lyons Press, 2010.

Angwin, Julia. *Dragnet Nation: A Quest for Privacy, Security, and Freedom in a World of Relentless Surveillance*. New York, NY: Macmillan, 2014.

Brenner, Joel. *Glass Houses: Privacy, Secrecy, and Cyber Insecurity in a Transparent World*. New York, NY: Penguin Books, 2013.

Clarke, Richard A. *Cyber War: The Next Threat to National Security and What to Do About It*. New York, NY: HarperCollins, 2010.

Greenwald, Glenn. *No Place to Hide: Edward Snowden, the NSA, and the U.S. Surveillance State*. New York, NY: Metropolitan Books, 2014.

Jenkins, Henry. *Convergence Culture: Where Old & New Media Collide*. New York, NY: New York University, 2006.

Jenkins, Henry. *Spreadable Media: Creating Value and Meaning in a Networked Culture*. New York, NY: New York University Press, 2013.

Jones, Alex. *Losing the News: The Future of the News That Feeds Democracy*. New York, NY: Oxford University Press, 2009.

Kaye, Jeff. *Funding Journalism in the Digital Age: Business Models, Strategies, Issues, and Trends*. New York, NY: Peter Lang, 2010.

Kovach, Bill, and Tom Rosenstiel. *Blur: How to Know What's True in the Age of Information Overload*. New York, NY: Bloomsbury, 2010.

Mayor-Schonberger, Viktor, and Kenneth Cukier. *Big Data: A Revolution That Will Transform How We Live, Work, and Think*. New York, NY: Houghton Mifflin Harcourt, 2013.

McChesney, Robert, and John Nichols. *The Death and Life of American Journalism: The Media Revolution That Will Begin the World Again*. New York, NY: Nation Books, 2010.

Rosenbaum, Steven. *Curation Nation: How to Win in a World Where Consumers Are Creators*. New York, NY: McGraw Hill, 2011.

Singer, P.W., and Allan Friedman. *Cybersecurity and Cyberwar: What Everyone Needs to Know*. Oxford, England: Oxford University Press, 2014.

Uscinski, Joseph E. *The People's News: Media, Politics, and the Demands of Capitalism*. New York, NY: New York University Press, 2014.

[1] Tate, Julie. "Judge Sentences Bradley Manning to 35 Years." *Washington Post*, August 21, 2013. Retrieved March 8, 2014 (http://www.washingtonpost.com/world/national-security/judge-to-sentence-bradley-manning-today/2013/08/20/85bee184-09d0-11e3-b87c-476db8ac34cd_story.html).

[2] Manning, Chelsea. "Sometimes You Have to Pay a Heavy Price to Live in a Free Society." *Common Dreams*, August 21, 2013. Retrieved March 8, 2014 (http://www.commondreams.org/view/2013/08/21-7).

[3] Smith, Gerry. "Scripps Employees Called 'Hackers' for Exposing Massive Security Flaw." *Huffington Post*, May 22, 2013. Retrieved March 8, 2014 (http://www.huffingtonpost.com/2013/05/22/scripps-reporters-hackers_n_3320701.html).

[4] Hsieh, Steven. "DOJ Drops Most of the Charges Against a Journalist Indicted for Sharing a Link." *The Nation*, March 5, 2014. Retrieved March 8, 2014 (http://www.thenation.com/blog/178711/doj-drops-most-charges-against-journalist-indicted-sharing-link#).

[5] King, Geoffrey. "Journalist Barrett Brown faces prison for publishing hyperlink." Committee to Protect Journalists, September 2013. Retrieved March 8, 2014 (https://www.cpj.org/Internet/2013/09/journalist-barrett-brown-faces-jail-for-posting-hy.php).

[6] "Wikileaks Cables: You Ask, We Search." *Guardian*. Retrieved March 18, 2014 (http://www.theguardian.com/world/series/wikileaks-cables-you-ask-we-search).

[7] "The Sarah Palin Emails." *Guardian*. Retrieved March 18, 2014 (http://www.theguardian.com/world/sarah-palin-emails?guni=Article:in%20body%20link).

[8] Caplan, Jeremy. "5 Ways to Crowdsource Easily, Legally, and with Quality." Poynter Institute, July 7, 2012. Retrieved March 18, 2014 (http://www.poynter.org/latest-news/top-stories/102533/5-ways-to-crowdsource-easily-legally-with-quality).

[9] Electronic Frontier Foundation. "Apple v. Does." 2006. Retrieved March 13, 2014 (https://www.eff.org/cases/apple-v-does).

[10] Robinson, Eric. "Bloggers and Shield Laws II: Now, You Can Worry." Digital

Media Law Project, January 26, 2012. Retrieved March 18, 2014 (http://www.dmlp.org/blog/2012/bloggers-and-shield-laws-ii-now-you-can-worry).

[11] Donovan, Lisa. "Jude Rules Technology Blogger Has No Right to Shield Confidential Source." *Chicago Sun-Times*, February 15, 2012. Retrieved March 18, 2014 (http://www.suntimes.com/9996433-417/judge-rules-technology-blogger-has-no-right-to-shield-confidential-source.html).

[12] McGregor, Susan. "How to Teach Digital Security to Journalists." PBS Idea Lab, February 6, 2014. Retrieved March 13, 2014 (http://www.pbs.org/idealab/2014/02/how-to-teach-digital-security-to-journalists).

[13] Aikins, Matthieu. "The Spy Who Came in from the Code: How a Filmmaker Accidentally Gave Up His Sources to Syrian Spooks." *Columbia Journalism Review*, May 3, 2012. Retrieved March 13, 2014 (http://www.cjr.org/feature/the_spy_who_came_in_from_the_c.php?page=all).

[14] Barr, Jeremy. "How Journalists Can Encrypt Their Email." Poynter Institute, December 30, 2013. Retrieved March 13, 2014 (http://www.poynter.org/how-tos/digital-strategies/234005/how-journalists-can-encrypt-their-email).

[15] Tor Project. "Tor: Overview." Retrieved March 14, 2014 (https://www.torproject.org/about/overview.html.en).

[16] Kirchner, Lauren. "Why Journalists Can Still Trust Tor." *Columbia Journalism Review*, October 8, 2013. Retrieved March 18, 2014 (http://www.cjr.org/behind_the_news/can_we_still_trust_tor.php?page=all).

[17] Gellman, Barton, Craig Timberg, and Steven Rich. "Secret NSA Documents Show Campaign Against Tor Encrypted Network." *Washington Post*, October 4, 2013. Retrieved March 18, 2014 (http://www.washingtonpost.com/world/national-security/secret-nsa-documents-show-campaign-against-tor-encrypted-network/2013/10/04/610f08b6-2d05-11e3-8ade-a1f23cda135e_story.html).

[18] Wyshywaniuk, Steve. "How Journalists Can Stay Secure Reporting from Android Devices." PBS Idea Lab, December 13, 2013. Retrieved March 23, 2014 (http://www.pbs.org/idealab/2013/12/how

-journalists-can-stay-secure-reporting-from-android-devices).

[19] Beck, Lindsay. "Phone Security: The Nosy Neighbor in Your Pocket." PBS Idea Lab, November 12, 2013. Retrieved March 18, 2014 (http://www.pbs.org/idealab/2013/11/phone-security-the-nosy-neighbor-in-your-pocket).

[20] Pitner, Barrett. "Digital Security, Email, and the New Cyber Frontier." PBS Idea Lab, January 23, 2014. Retrieved March 18, 2014 (http://www.pbs.org/idealab/2014/01/digital-security-email-and-the-new-cyber-frontier).

[21] United States Department of Justice. "Freedom of Information Act Exemptions." Retrieved March 18, 2014 (http://www.justice.gov/oip/foia-exemptions.pdf).

[22] Burke, Lindsay. "Federal Court Finds Store Communications Act Applies to Facebook Wall Posts." Digital Media Law Project, September 10, 2013. Retrieved March 18, 2014 (http://www.dmlp.org/blog/2013/federal-court-finds-stored-communications-act-applies-facebook-wall-posts).

[23] Kirchner, Lauren. "Teaching J-School Students Cyber-Security." Columbia Journalism Review, November 15, 2013. Retrieved March 18, 2014 (http://www.cjr.org/behind_the_news/teaching_cybersecurity_in_jsch.php?page=all).

[24] Gallagher, Ryan. "Timeline: How the World Was Misled About Government Skype Eavesdropping." Slate, July 12, 2013. Retrieved March 18, 2014 (http://www.slate.com/blogs/future_tense/2013/07/12/skype_surveillance_a_timeline_of_public_claims_and_private_government_dealings.html).

[25] Rogers, Kate. "Facebook's Messenger Lawsuit: Data Mining 'Dislike.'" Fox Business, 2014. Retrieved March 21, 2014 (http://www.foxbusiness.com/personal-finance/2014/01/03/facebooks-messenger-lawsuit-data-mining-dislike).

[26] Facebook Data Use Policy. "Information We Receive and How It Is Used." Retrieved March 21, 2014 (https://www.facebook.com/about/privacy/your-info).

[27] "Street View: Google Given 35 Days to Delete Wi-Fi Data." BBC News, June

21, 2013. Retrieved March 21, 2014 (http://www.bbc.com/news/technology-23002166#story_continues_2).

28 Mears, Bill, and Evan Perez. "Judge: NSA Domestic Phone Data-Mining Unconstitutional." CNN, December 16, 2013. Retrieved March 23, 2014 (http://www.cnn.com/2013/12/16/justice/nsa-surveillance-court-ruling).

29 Sheehy, Kelsey. "4 Questions Parents Should Ask About Student Data Security." *U.S. News & World Report*, January 13, 2014. Retrieved March 23, 2014 (http://www.usnews.com/education/blogs/high-school-notes/2014/01/13/4-questions-parents-should-ask-about-student-data-security).

30 Reidenberg, Joel, N. Cameron Russell, Jordan Kovnot, Thomas B. Norton, Ryan Cloutier, and Daniela Alvarado. "Privacy and Cloud Computing in Public Schools." Center on Law and Information Policy, Book 2, 2013. Retrieved March 23, 2014 (http://ir.lawnet.fordham.edu/clip/2).

31 Bogle, Ariel. "Study: Student Data not Safe in the Cloud." *Slate*, December 16, 2013. Retrieved March 23, 2014 (http://www.slate.com/blogs/future_tense/2013/12/16/fordham_center_on_law_and_information_policy_study_student_data_not_safe.html).

32 Strauss, Valerie. "Privacy Concerns Grow Over Gates-Funded Student Database." *Washington Post* Blog, June 9, 2013. Retrieved March 23, 2014 (http://www.washingtonpost.com/blogs/answer-sheet/wp/2013/06/09/privacy-concerns-grow-over-gates-funded-student-database/?print=1).

33 Smyth, Frank. "Digital Security Basics for Journalists." Medill National Security Zone. Retrieved March 18, 2014 (http://nationalsecurityzone.org/site/digital-security-basics-for-journalists/#basics).

34 "Journalist Security Guide." Committee to Protect Journalists. Retrieved March 18, 2014 (http://www.cpj.org/reports/2012/04/journalist-security-guide.php).

35 Kirchner, Lauren. "Teaching J-School Students Cyber-Security." *Columbia*

Journalism Review, November 15, 2013. Retrieved March 18, 2014 (http://www.cjr.org/behind_the_news/teaching_cybersecurity_in_jsch .php?page=all).

[36] Ordonez, Sandra. "11 Steps Toward Better Digital Hygiene." PBS Idea Lab, November 6, 2013. Retrieved March 18, 2014 (http://www.pbs.org/ idealab/2013/11/11-steps-toward-better-digital-hygiene).

[37] Talbot, David. "A $629 Ultrasecure Phone Aims to Protect Personal Data." *MIT Technology Review*, February 24, 2014. Retrieved March 23, 2014 (http://www.technologyreview.com/news/524906/a-629-ultrasecure- phone-aims-to-protect-personal-data).

[38] Simonite, Tom. "For $3,500, a Spy-Resistant Smartphone." *MIT Technology Review*, March 18, 2014. Retrieved March 23, 2014 (http:// www.technologyreview.com/news/525556/for-3500-a-spy -resistant-smartphone).

[39] Lidzborski, Nicolas. "Staying at the Forefront of Email Security and Reliability: HTTPS-Only and 99.978% Availability." Gmail Blog, March 20, 2014. Retrieved March 23, 2014 (http://gmailblog.blogspot.de/2014/03/ staying-at-forefront-of-email-security.html).

[40] Pagliery, Jose. "Google Tries to NSA-Proof Gmail." CNN Money, March 21, 2014. Retrieved March 23, 2014 (http://money.cnn.com/2014/ 03/20/technology/security/gmail-nsa/index.html?iid=SF_T_River).

INDEX

S

secure technology, future of, 31–32
security, politics of, 18–21
shield law protections, 10–11
Skype, 22–23
smartphone connections, securing,
    16–18, 31
Smyth, Frank, 28
Snowden, Edward, 4, 5, 12, 13,
    16, 22, 25
social media, privacy settings on, 29, 31
sources, protecting, 10–11, 13

Stored Communications Act, 21
student data, surveillance and mining of,
    25–27

T

Tor, 15–16, 17
two-step verification, 29, 30–31

W

web browsing, anonymous, 11, 31, 36–37
WikiLeaks, 5, 8
Wood, Brock, interview with,
    33–37

ABOUT THE AUTHOR

Megan Fromm is an assistant professor at Boise State University and faculty for the Salzburg Academy on Media & Global Change, a summer media literacy study-abroad program. She is also the professional support director for the Journalism Education Association.

Fromm received her Ph.D. in 2010 from the Philip Merrill College of Journalism at the University of Maryland. Her dissertation analyzed how news media frame student First Amendment court cases, particularly those involving freedom of speech and press. Her work and teaching centers on media law, scholastic journalism, media literacy, and media and democracy. She has also worked as a journalist and high school journalism teacher. Fromm has taught at Johns Hopkins University, Towson University, the University of Maryland, and the Newseum.

As a working journalist, Fromm won numerous awards, including the Society of Professional Journalists Sunshine Award and the Colorado Friend of the First Amendment Award. Fromm worked in student media through high school and college and interned at the Student Press Law Center in 2004. Her career in journalism began at Grand Junction High School (Grand Junction, Colorado), where she was a reporter and news editor for the award-winning student newspaper, the *Orange & Black*.

PHOTO CREDITS